MANITOBA

JOURNEY ACROSS CANADA

Harry Beckett

The Rourke Book Co., Inc.
Vero Beach, Florida 32964

Harry Beckett M.A. (Cambridge), M. Ed. (Toronto), Dip. Ed. (Hull, England) has taught at the elementary and high school levels in England, Canada, France, and Germany. He has also travelled widely for a tour operator and a major book company.

Edited by Laura Edlund
Laura Edlund received her B.A. in English literature from the University of Toronto and studied Writing for Multimedia and Book Editing and Design at Centennial College. She has been an editor since 1986 and a traveller always.

ACKNOWLEDGMENTS
For photographs: Geovisuals (Kitchener, Ontario), The Canadian Tourism Commission and its photographers.
For reference: *The Canadian Encyclopedia, Encarta 1997, The Canadian Global Almanac, Symbols of Canada. Canadian Heritage*, Reproduced with the permission of the Minister of Public Works and Government Services Canada, 1997.
For maps: Promo-Grafx of Collingwood, Ont., Canada.

Library of Congress Cataloging-in-Publication Data

Beckett, Harry. 1936 -
   Manitoba / by Harry Beckett.
     p. cm. — (Journey across Canada)
   Includes index.
   Summary: An introduction to the geography, history, economy, major cities, and interesting sites of the province that is the geographic center of Canada.
   ISBN 1-55916-203-1
   1. Manitoba—Juvenile literature. [1. Manitoba] I. Title.
II. Series: Beckett. Harry, 1936- Journey across Canada.
F1062.4.B43 1997
971.27—dc21   97-7672
                                           CIP
                                           AC

TABLE OF CONTENTS

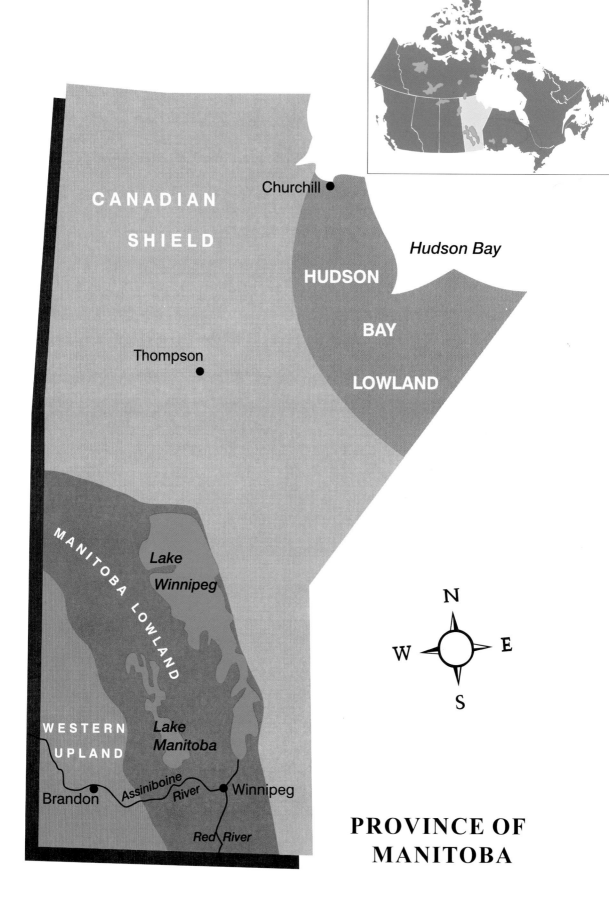

CANADIAN

SHIELD

Churchill ●

HUDSON

Hudson Bay

BAY

LOWLAND

Thompson
●

MANITOBA LOWLAND

Lake
Winnipeg

N

W ○ E

S

WESTERN

UPLAND

Lake
Manitoba

Brandon ●   Assiniboine   River   ● Winnipeg

Red River

**PROVINCE OF
MANITOBA**

Chapter One

SIZE AND LOCATION

Manitoba is the geographic centre of Canada. Because of its position linking eastern and western Canada, Manitoba has been called the "keystone" province. A keystone is the stone at the top of an arch that balances the sides and holds the other stones in place.

When the province was created in 1870, Manitoba was a tiny rectangle where the Red and Assiniboine rivers meet. It was extended twice before it reached its present size in 1912. The province stretches 793 kilometres (493 miles) from its border with the states of Minnesota and North Dakota in the south, to Hudson Bay and the 60th **parallel** (PER uh lel) in the north. In the south, Manitoba extends 447 kilometres (278 miles) from Saskatchewan in the west to Ontario in the east.

Find out more...

- Manitoba is 649 950 square kilometres (250 965 square miles) in area.
- Manitoba's coastline on Hudson Bay is 917 kilometres (570 miles) long.
- The southern border is the 49th parallel.

Chapter Two

GEOGRAPHY: LAND AND WATER

The Hudson Bay Lowland and the **Canadian Shield** (kuh NAY dee un SHEELD) make up two thirds of Manitoba.

The Lowland is extremely cold, with **permafrost** (PUR muh frost) under thin soil. The Shield has low hills, forests, lakes, and rocky outcrops. Both areas have bushes and bogs, which are a type of swamp or marsh. Few people live in these regions.

The Canadian Shield, a land of rock, forests, and lakes

The Red River winds its way north towards Winnipeg.

Beside the Shield is a low, flat plain that was once the bed of a lake. It covers a fifth of the province. From this area, the land rises. In the southwest corner of the province, the Western Upland is cut by wide valleys.

Manitoba has several major rivers. Most flow through lakes Winnipeg, Manitoba, or Winnipegosis into Hudson Bay. A flood on the Red River in 1997 was called the "Flood of the Century."

Chapter Three

WHAT IS THE WEATHER LIKE?

People say that the street corner of Portage and Main in Winnipeg is the coldest in Canada.

Manitoba lies quite far north and away from any oceans. Cold air flows down from the Arctic. As a result, the winters are very cold. The snowfall seems to be heavier than it is because it stays on the ground all winter.

As warm air begins to flow from the south, spring arrives first in the Red River Valley and moves slowly north and west.

The summers become warm, except in the north, where they remain cool. The rain is light. It falls mostly in the growing season.

Find out more...

- This climate, with extreme summer and winter temperatures, is called a continental climate.
- Winnipeg gets an average 115 centimetres (45 inches) of snow each year. Churchill, in the north, gets 200 centimetres (79 inches).

Manitobans enjoying winter in Riding Mountain National Park

Chapter Four

Manitoba's farmland is in the lowland and upland of the southwest, where the soil is rich, and the growing season, long. The lowland needs to be drained, **irrigated** (IR uh gate ud), and protected against floods for successful farming.

The main crop is wheat, followed by barley, oats, and canola. **Livestock** (LIVE stok) production is next to wheat in importance. Beef cattle are raised on the grasslands of the southwest, and dairy herds, hogs, and poultry in the southeast.

Market gardening and dairy farming around Winnipeg supply the city's needs. To the east, Native peoples collect wild rice and medicinal herbs in Whiteshell Provincial Park.

Forestry and fishing are very small industries in Manitoba.

A row of grain elevators in Winkler, Manitoba

Find out more...

- Wheat is five times as important as barley and oats together.
- Over 4 million hectares (9.88 million acres) are planted with field crops.

11

Chapter Five

FROM THE EARLIEST PEOPLES

The first European explorers of Manitoba came to the Hudson Bay coast. They were looking for the Northwest Passage to the Pacific Ocean and for furs.

For 200 years Native peoples, the French and English people of the Hudson's Bay and the North West trading companies, and the **Métis** (MAY tee) trapped and traded furs.

The first settlers' houses were built of sod.

The grave site of the Métis leader, Louis Riel

In 1812, Lord Selkirk created the Red River Colony, the first European farming community. As farming spread, it created conflicts with Native peoples, including the Métis.

Britain bought Manitoba, or Rupert's Land as it was called, in 1870 from the Hudson's Bay Company. It then became Canada's fifth province.

Between 1878 and 1881, free land attracted 40 000 new settlers.

Chapter Six

MAKING A LIVING: FROM INDUSTRY

The Canadian Shield is rich in minerals. Manitoba supplies a third of Canada's nickel, as well as gold, copper, zinc, and tantalum.

Manufacturing is the most important industry. It often uses the province's natural resources to make prepared foods, metal products, transportation equipment, and newsprint. There is plenty of electricity to power these industries.

Manitoba is at the heart of Canada's transportation network. The Canadian National and Canadian Pacific railways and the trans-Canada oil pipeline pass through the province.

Many people work in service industries—government, trade, banking, education, and tourism.

Find out more...

- Thompson has the biggest mining, smelting, and refining plant in North America.

- Manitoba has good access to the United States and, through Churchill, to other international destinations.

A railway repair yard

Chapter Seven

IF YOU GO THERE...

The Winnipeg area has many attractions. Lower Fort Garry is a restored Hudson's Bay Company fort, and the Forks is a waterfront recreational, cultural, historic, and business centre where the Red and Assiniboine rivers meet. People have lived and traded at the Forks for 6000 years.

Winnipeg's varied communities hold many festivals, including Folklorama, the world's largest celebration of **ethnic** (ETH nik) groups.

In the southwest, Riding Mountain National Park draws thousands of tourists to see wolves and elks, and to enjoy its lakes and campsites.

In the fall, polar bears gather along the Hudson Bay shore to hunt seals, and Churchill becomes the polar bear capital of the world. History is recreated in Churchill's partially rebuilt Prince of Wales Fort.

A polar bear near Churchill

Find out more...

- Manitoba's Children's Museum is at the Forks.
- The Royal Canadian Mint in Winnipeg is a popular spot.

Chapter Eight
MAJOR CITIES

Winnipeg is called the "Gateway to the West," where the Canadian Shield ends and the **prairies** (PRARE eez) begin. It is the capital of Manitoba and the centre of a rail, road, and river network. Winnipeg is home to 57% of the province's population and most of its industry and trade.

A tour boat on Winnipeg's Red River. The Legislature is on the left.

The Royal Canadian Mint in Winnipeg doesn't give samples!

The city is proud of its Royal Ballet, museums, and ethnic communities. St.-Boniface, a Winnipeg suburb, is a historic French community.

Brandon, on the Canadian Pacific Railway, is the main city serving the southwest. It is an important industrial centre with a university. Brandon has hosted the Canada Winter and Summer Games and the World Curling Championships.

Chapter Nine

SIGNS AND SYMBOLS

The flag is the Red Ensign with the provincial shield to the side. The shield shows the cross of St. George of England and a buffalo, an important animal for Native peoples and early settlers.

The coat of arms shows the shield and other symbols. The gold helmet signals Manitoba's status in Canada. The beaver is the Canadian emblem and the crocus, the provincial flower. The unicorn on the left recalls the province's Scottish settlers, and the horse, on the right, was vital to Native peoples and early settlers. They stand among water, grain fields, and forests.

The Latin motto means "Glorious and free."

The provincial flower is the prairie crocus, which is often seen as the last snows melt.

Manitoba's flag, coat of arms, and flower

GLOSSARY

Canadian Shield (kuh NAY dee un SHEELD) —
a horseshoe-shaped area of rock covering about
half of Canada

ethnic (ETH nik) — of various groups of people
and their characteristics, cultures, and languages

irrigate (IR uh gate) — to bring water to land
using ditches, sprinklers, etc.

livestock (LIVE stok) — farm animals

Métis (MAY tee) — French, meaning person of
mixed blood, especially descending from French
and Native ancestry in prairie river valleys

permafrost (PUR muh frost) — ground that is
always frozen at, or just below, the surface

prairies (PRARE eez) — plains of southern
Manitoba, Saskatchewan, and Alberta

parallel (PER uh lel) — a line on a map joining
points at the same distance from the equator

*A Ukrainian-Canadian family painting pysanka (Easter eggs)
in Winnipeg.*